THE MANUAL

21st Century Edition

RELATED BOOKS
FROM SAM TORODE

AS A MAN THINKETH
21st Century Edition

THE MEDITATIONS
An Emperor's Guide to Mastery

LIVING FROM THE SOUL
*The 7 Spiritual Principles
of Ralph Waldo Emerson*

SECRETS OF THE MIND
*Ralph Waldo Emerson's Keys
to Expansive Mental Powers*

TAO TE CHING
The Book of the Way

THE MANUAL

21st CENTURY EDITION

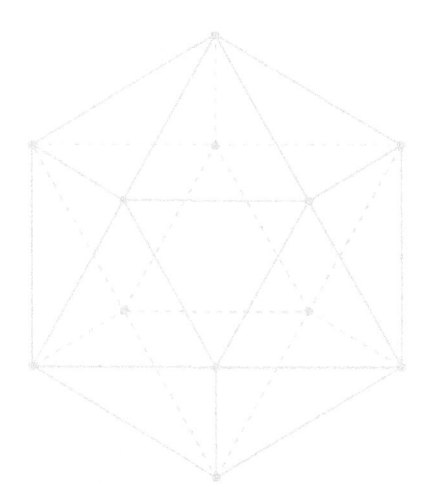

EPICTETUS
paraphrased by SAM TORODE

Rendered in contemporary language by Sam Torode,
loosely based on the 1866 translation by Thomas Wentworth Higginson.
Copyright © 2021 Sam Torode.
All rights reserved.

Published by Ancient Renewal,
an imprint of Sam Torode Book Arts
www.samtorode.com

FOREWORD

We live in a crazy world. Every day we're bombarded with news of mass shootings, extreme weather and climate change, racism and discrimination, corporate corruption, economic inequality, political polarization, attacks on democracy, and authoritarianism on the rise.

The internet, which promised to put all the world's knowledge at our fingertips, has been weaponized by con artists and conspiracists. Social media, which promised to bring us together, has divided us into echo chambers and made us more vulnerable to propaganda.

To distract from the news we scroll Instagram, and wind up feeling like everyone's life is beautiful and perfect except ours. Is it any wonder that depression and anxiety are epidemic?

Oh—and then there's the global pandemic, which is taking thousands of lives per day as I write this.

Would you believe that two thousand years ago, a group of Greek and Roman philosophers thought that *they* lived in a crazy world, too? They looked around and saw natural disasters, poverty, slavery, political corruption, injustice, and—yes—pandemics. They saw people numbing their pain with wine and cheering as gladiators battled each other to the death. (Is that so different from our sports bars?)

These philosophers were called Stoics, because the founder of their school, Zeno (c. 334–262 BCE), held classes on a porch surrounded by columns—a *stoa*, in Greek. Several hundred years after Zeno, a former slave named Epictetus (c. 50-135 CE) emerged as the most insightful and influential teacher of Stoicism.

The Stoics were concerned with finding peace of mind in the midst of chaos and uncertainty. You can't change the world, they realized—but you *can* change the way you look at the world and how you react to it.

The Manual is a collection of Epictetus' best teachings, compiled by one of his students. I first encountered *The Manual* in 2008, at a low point in my life. Putting Epictetus' advice into practice carried me through my darkest days. More than a book of philosophy, it's a handbook for living.

In 2017, I took Thomas Wentworth Higginson's 1866 translation of *The Manual*, rephrased it in contemporary

English, and published it. Though I updated the language to make it easier to understand, my version stayed very close to the original.

This year, I decided to revisit and completely rewrite *The Manual* with high school and college students in mind. In some places I trimmed; in others I elaborated. The result is a looser, amplified translation aimed at conveying the message of Epictetus for our times.

My hope is that this new edition of *The Manual* will help you find the inner wellspring of peace, purpose, and happiness—and so bring a little more sanity into this crazy, beautiful world.

—Sam Torode
October, 2021

Your Sphere of Power

There are things that are within your power, and things that are beyond your power. The key is learning to distinguish between the two.

Within your power are your opinions, desires (the things you pursue), aversions (the things you avoid), and how you treat other people. In sum, *your own thoughts and actions.*

Beyond your power are the thoughts and actions of others, your family and nationality, the physical characteristics you were born with, and all that fate may give or take from you.

Within your sphere of power, you're free, independent, and strong. Outside that sphere, you're constrained, dependent, and weak.

If you pin your hopes on things outside your control, you're likely to end up miserable, blaming others and cursing fate.

But if you focus only on what's within your power, then you're in charge. When you take responsibility for your own thoughts and actions, there's no one to blame or fight.

Do you want to be peaceful and content? Then release your attachment to everything beyond your control. This is the only path to freedom and happiness.

If you want peace *but also power*, or contentment *but also wealth*, you're likely to lose the former in pursuit of the latter.

Remember that your thoughts are not *facts*; they're *interpretations*. Whenever something upsets you, ask, "Is this inside or outside my sphere of power?" And if it's beyond your power to control, let it go.

2
Desire & Aversion

Desire drives you to *acquire* things. Aversion drives you to *avoid* things. When you don't get what you want, you're disappointed. When you get what you don't want, you're distressed.

When you strive to attain or avoid things that are beyond your control, you inflict mental anguish upon yourself.

Learn to direct your desire and aversion to things that are within your power, and take a neutral attitude to everything else. Then you'll be content.

For instance, instead of desiring fame and wealth, desire to improve your character and work ethic. And instead of worrying about sickness or death, take up healthy habits and release your fear.

First, secure your sphere of power. *Then* you may pursue something outside your control—such as entering a competition—with the calm determination to give it your best effort. If you win, you won't gloat or taunt your opponents, and if you lose, you'll still walk away with your head held high.

3
See Things as They Are

What about the possessions you enjoy, or the people that you love? Since they're outside your control, should you treat them indifferently?

No, it's good to love and appreciate the blessings in your life! Just remind yourself of their *nature* as physical objects or mortal beings.

When you drink from your favorite cup, remember that it's *made of clay*. It can't last forever. If it breaks, you needn't be upset.

When you hug your loved ones, remember that they're *mortal*. Accept the inevitability of death rather than denying it. Then, should they pass on before you, you'll find the strength to bear it.

4
The Nature of Things

Likewise, when you prepare for any event, remind yourself of its nature.

For instance, before going to the public pool, think of what usually happens—people are noisy, kids are splashing, and items left unattended are liable to be stolen. Set your expectations accordingly, and you won't be disappointed.

If something undesirable happens—such as, a child splashes you in the face—remind yourself, "My desire is to stay in harmony with the nature of things. And that child's nature is to splash."

5
Opinions

People aren't upset by *things themselves*, but by the *opinions* they have of those things.

Even death itself is nothing to fear. The fear of death comes from the *opinion* that death is a horrific tragedy to be avoided at all costs.

Socrates had a different opinion. He viewed death as a *return to the source*. He chose to die rather than betray his principles, which—to him—would have been the *real* tragedy.

Whenever you're upset, angry, or sad, don't blame anyone else. Your state of mind comes from your own opinions and interpretations.

Those who are *ignorant* of philosophy blame others for their own condition. Those who are *beginning* to learn philosophy blame themselves. Those who are *advanced* in philosophy blame no one.

6
Possessions

Don't take pride in your possessions—they're not really yours.

If a horse were to say, "Look at me—I'm so handsome!" his vanity would be excusable.

But if *you* brag, "I have the handsomest horse in the land!" you're claiming merit that doesn't belong to you.

What's really yours? All of your *thoughts, words, and actions*. When these are in harmony, you can take just satisfaction.

7
Stay Alert

Imagine you're taking a sea voyage. While the ship is anchored and you go ashore for supplies, you may amuse yourself by looking for beautiful shells and stones on the beach.

But always keep part of your mind focused on the ship, staying alert for the captain's call. Be prepared to give up your "treasures" at any moment, or you may miss the boat!

So in life, remain steadfast in pursuit of your mission, always willing to drop distractions.

8
Be Flexible

Don't wish that all things will go well with you, but that *you will go well* with all things.

9
Obstacles

Lameness may strike your leg, but not your determination. Sickness may weaken your body, but not your character. Misfortune may drain your bank account, but not your generosity—unless you let it.

Each time an obstacle arises, remind yourself of this truth: while it may hurt some part of you, it can't touch *your deepest self*.

The only person who can truly harm you—that is, make you a worse person—is *you*.

10
Exercising Virtue

Whenever you face a challenge, turn inward and ask, "What virtue can I use in this situation?"

If you meet temptation, exercise *self control*. If you meet pain, exercise *perseverance*. If you meet frustration, exercise *patience*.

By doing this repeatedly, you'll gain strength to overcome life's challenges rather than be overcome *by* them.

11
Everything Is on Loan

Don't say of anything, "I've lost it," but rather, "I've given it back."

Did my cup fall and shatter? *I've given it back.*

Did my jewelry get stolen? *I've given it back.*

Did my grandmother pass away? *I've given her back.*

Treat everything as if it were on loan, because *it is*.

Eventually, all things must return to their divine Source. The method and timing of their return is not up to you.

12
No More Excuses

If you want to move forward, stop making excuses.

"But if I don't cling to my possessions, someone will steal them! And If I don't worry about money, I'll end up on the street!"

Enough with the catastrophizing. What's better—to die poor yet *free from fear*, or to live surrounded by riches yet *filled with anxiety*?

Start with small things. If a bottle of wine is broken or goes missing, remind yourself, "Accepting such annoyances is the price of my peace of mind."

Or if a friend lets you down, remember that they're responsible for their own actions. Why give them the power to upset you?

13
Insults & Accolades

As you embark on the path of philosophy, don't mind what others may think about you—even if they call you foolish. Don't expect to be praised for pursuing inner peace.

And if you *are* praised by others, be skeptical of yourself. It's no easy feat to hold onto your inner harmony while collecting accolades! When grasping for one, you're likely to drop the other.

14
Unrealistic Expectations

It's foolish to expect your family and friends to live forever. Their lives are not in your power.

It's also foolish to expect them to be perfect and always please you. Don't wish someone to be something they're not.

Whenever you strongly desire something that's beyond your control, you set yourself up for disappointment. To avoid disappointment, direct your desires to things that are *within your sphere of power*.

If you wish to be free, don't pin your happiness on anyone else.

15
The Banquet of LIfe

Approach life as a banquet.

As each platter is passed to you, sample it with gratitude. If you're waiting for your favorite dish to come around, don't lunge across the table for it—be patient.

And if the plate is empty when it reaches you, don't grumble. Instead, be glad that others were able to enjoy it.

If you treat everything this way, you'll be worthy to feast with the gods!

16
Stories We Tell Ourselves

Learn to distinguish between *events* and *interpretations*. Events themselves do not upset us. Rather, it's the stories we tell ourselves about those events.

One athlete is distraught over a setback and gives up; while another is spurred on, eager to overcome the challenge.

When you see someone crying, ask yourself: what story is behind their tears? If they looked at things from a different perspective, would it change their feelings?

Don't share your thoughts with the grieving person, unless asked. Only sympathize with them, and perhaps even cry with them. You can shed tears outwardly, while inwardly remaining at peace.

17
Life Is a Stage

Think of life as a play, and yourself as an actor. The role you play, and the amount of time you have on the stage, is not up to you—it's up to the Author.

You may be cast as a pauper, a cripple, or a king. You don't get to choose the era, nationality, class, family, or body into which you're born.

But you alone have the power to act well in your role. Play your part to the best of your ability!

18
Make Your Own Luck

If you break a mirror or a black cat crosses your path, don't be afraid of bad luck and create a self-fulfilling prophecy. "Bad omens" have no power *unless we give it to them*.

Assure yourself, "All signs point to good luck if I interpret them that way. I'll find the advantage in everything that comes my way."

19
Acceptance

If you learn to *accept* all things outside your control, instead of *resisting* them, you'll be unshakable.

When you see a person who's rich, famous, or powerful, don't be fooled by appearances and assume that they're happy.

When you focus on cultivating your own virtue, there's no room for envying or imitating others. Instead of desiring to be a billionaire, a celebrity, or a president, *desire to be free*.

And the way to be free is to work within your sphere of power, taking everything else as it comes.

20
Revise Your Story

When someone upsets you, remember that it's actually *your own opinion* that upsets you.

It's not the person who criticized or attacked you that torments your mind, but the *story you tell yourself about what happened.*

Don't get stuck on the first story that enters your mind. Give it time and take a wider perspective, and you'll regain inner peace.

21
Use Your Time Wisely

Every day, remind yourself that you're a mortal being and your time on Earth is limited.

Instead of depressing you, this is meant to *inspire* you to use your precious time wisely, and not waste it in chasing after possessions or stewing over grievances.

22
Dealing with Criticism

If you intend to follow the path of philosophy, expect your family and friends to misunderstand or mock you.

"Well, well, look who's a philosopher now!" they might say. Or, "So you think you're better than us?"

Don't argue or take on an air of superiority. Simply stay focused on your inner work, while performing your outer work—at school, in your job, wherever you are—to the best of your ability.

If you abandon the path to please others, you might avoid criticism but betray yourself.

23
Respect Yourself

Whenever you find yourself acting to impress others, or stopping out of fear of what others might think, you've left the path.

Find satisfaction in seeking wisdom and cultivating virtue—not in praise and honors.

If you want to be respected, start by respecting yourself!

Seeking Significance

"I'll never be anybody. I'm just a nobody from nowhere."

Don't fret about your significance or how you'll be remembered. Instead of striving for fame and renown, find your significance *within yourself*.

"But I want fame so that I can reach a large audience and help others."

What do you mean by "help"? Can you really give them happiness and peace of mind? That's within *their* sphere of power, not yours. And even if it were possible—how can you give someone a gift that you, yourself, don't have?

"But I'll make lots of money and then give it away."

If you can accumulate riches without sacrificing your honor and self-respect, then do it. But if you compromise your principles in the process, no amount of money can make up for lost virtue.

Which would you rather have—money to give away, or loyal and trustworthy friends? The two don't often go together.

To become the kind of person who attracts good friends, build your character—not your bank account.

"Then what's my role in the world?"

The one in which you can best express your talents and skills, which are within your sphere of power. Everyone has a vital role to play—you're already important, right where you are.

25
Everything Has Its Price

Do you envy someone who's popular and gets invited to all the best parties? If they're admired for their *virtues*, be glad for them. But if they're celebrated for their *vices*, be glad you're not like them.

When you see someone who's beloved by many, notice the effort they put into building relationships. If you want to *have* good friends, you must *be* a good friend.

Everything has its price. If you aren't invited to a party, it's probably because you haven't spent time befriending, flattering, or doing favors for the hosts. Is that a price you're willing to pay?

No invitation is worth praising people you don't really admire and making small talk with people you don't really like.

26
An Outside View

If your neighbor's child shattered their precious vase, you'd take the news in stride, saying, "Oh well, accidents happen."

But how would you react if it was *your* precious vase? Would you cry over the broken pieces? Fly into a rage?

Why the difference? You ought to react with calmness and understanding in *both* cases.

Whenever misfortune befalls you, take an outside view of things. Ask yourself—how would I respond if *someone else* were in this situation?

27
The Target

Goodness stands before us like an archer's target.

Evil has no positive existence; it's merely the *lack* of goodness. Sin is a missing of the mark—an arrow gone astray.

28
Mental Bondage

If someone tried to control your body, you'd fight for freedom.

But how easily you hand over your *mind* to those who offend or insult you! By continually stewing over their misdeeds, you make them your master.

29
Be Well Prepared

When approaching any situation, consider all three phases—*before, during,* and *after*. Only then take action. If you act without taking the causes and consequences into account, you'll flounder and fail.

Let's say you want to enter a wrestling tournament. What comes before? You must train hard, eat well, and listen to your coach.

What might happen during and after the tournament? Devise a game plan for all contingencies, including possible injury and loss.

Once you've considered all this, if you still want to compete, start training. But if you haven't seriously thought things through, you're only fantasizing.

Becoming a philosopher, like becoming a wrestler, takes practice. It isn't a hobby to be dabbled in and abandoned when the going gets tough.

A lot of people who fancy themselves philosophers are mere imitators. They've changed their way of dressing and speaking—*but not their thinking*. They can repeat wise words, but on the inside, their minds are cauldrons of fear and envy.

If you truly wish to be a philosopher, you must gain disciple and self-control, give up friends who are bad influences, stop striving for power, riches, and fame, and willingly accept ridicule and scorn.

Are you eager to make these sacrifices for peace, freedom, and inner harmony? If so, start training!

30
Duty & Dignity

All relationships come with reciprocal duties.

Parents have the duty to love, care for, and teach their children. Children have the duty of following their parents' instruction, receiving their correction, and caring for them in their old age.

What if your parent gives you bad advice, or treats you unfairly—are your duties cancelled?

Before judging *their* behavior—which you can't control—examine *your own*. Fulfill your duties as best you can without compromising your dignity and inner harmony.

If you must disobey or disappoint a parent, do it with a kind spirit and a clear conscience. Remember—no one can steal your peace of mind unless you let them.

31
Worship

To know the gods, study the *ways of nature*. Follow them, let them shape you, and be guided by their perfect wisdom. Stay close to nature, and you'll never feel far from the gods.

Go with the flow of nature by letting go of all things beyond your control. Don't judge the things that come your way as "good" or "bad"—only judge your own thoughts, desires, and actions.

If you fight the flow by arguing with events and circumstances outside your control, you'll end up cursing the gods. For if you believe the gods would deliberately try to harm you, how could you worship them?

Where your *love* is, there is your *worship*. Religion isn't something set apart from the rest of life. Worship the gods in humility and simplicity by embracing nature's ways.

32
Listen to Nature

It's helpful to anticipate future events and plan for them; but don't let what might happen *tomorrow* make you fearful or anxious *today*.

The future is beyond your control; but it's within your power to approach it with an open and peaceful mind.

Remember that outside events can't touch your deepest self—what matters is how you *interpret* and *react* to them. With the right mindset, you can use any circumstance to your benefit.

Trust fate, and trust yourself. Take counsel from nature, not from prophets and prognosticators.

Suppose you visit a fortune teller, and she predicts that one of your friends will betray you. Will you let this change your behavior, by abandoning your friend before they can abandon you? Then you create a self-fulfilling prophecy.

Nature teaches that we're all connected and interdependent. Being a loyal friend is its own reward—it makes you a better person—even if your friends sometimes let you down. What other oracle do you need?

33
Social Etiquette

Be the same person in public as in private.

Be a good listener, not a loudmouth or bore. Speak only what's constructive and enriching.

Don't participate in gossip. When people start criticizing and complaining, change the subject or leave the room.

Avoid degrading entertainment. If your friends keep inviting you to watch such shows, find new friends or you'll soon find yourself off the path and in a mud pit.

When you attend sporting events, don't let the outcome determine your mood. Appreciate all the athletes' efforts, and wish only that the best will win.

At parties, be a polite guest. Don't revel to the point of losing your dignity.

If you're not sure how to act, just ask yourself—what would Socrates do? Model yourself after the wisest.

34
Temptation

When you're burning with desire, you're like a person under a spell.

Instead of acting on impulse, take a step back. Consider the costs of pursuing this pleasure and what consequences may follow. Ask yourself, "If I indulge now, how will I feel about myself tomorrow?"

Then ask, "How will I feel about myself if I *resist* this temptation?"

Asking these questions will break the spell. The enchantment will fade, and you'll see things as they really are.

If you decide that a certain pleasure is wholesome and harmless, enjoy it in moderation.

Self-respect is more satisfying than any bodily pleasure.

35
Act Decisively

Once you've thought through the consequences, act decisively. Don't worry about what others will think, even if the whole world might misunderstand you.

If you wind up off course, correct yourself. But if you know did the right thing, why fear those who misjudge you?

36
The Scale of Values

Black and white thinking makes for powerful speeches, but real life is mostly shades of gray. It's rarely a question of good versus evil, but of weighing greater and lesser goods on a scale of values.

At a banquet, taking all the choice cuts may be good for your belly, but sharing generously is good for the spirit of celebration. Weighing the two goods, seeing your fellow guests enjoy themselves is more valuable than gratifying your own appetite.

37
Authentic Living

The best line of work is the one best suited to your unique gifts.

If you pretend to be someone you're not, you might gain fame, riches, or political power—but you'll miss out on the joys of a life spent expressing your true thoughts, temperament, and talents.

38
Watch Your Step

When walking in the woods, watch for sharp stones and fallen branches in your path.

So, too, when thinking—take care not to stumble into illogic and unreason.

39
Fitting Possessions

Our possessions should be suited to our needs, just as our shoes are suited to our feet.

Could you run faster if your shoes were *larger* than your feet, or gold-plated and diamond studded? Of course not.

Once you let your appetite exceed what's necessary and helpful, desire knows no bounds.

40
True Beauty

Some people confuse their self-worth with their ability to attract the opposite sex, and so pour all their energies into physical appearance—makeup, clothing, jewelry, and the like.

If only they realized that *virtue*, *honor*, and *self-respect* are the marks of true beauty!

41
What's on the Inside

When a person is overly focused on bodily things—obsessing over food, endlessly exercising, or spending hours grooming—it betrays the poverty of their interior life.

Care for your body as needed, but put most of your energy towards *cultivating your mind*.

Warped Perspective

When someone hinders or criticizes you, remember that they can only see you through the lens of their own impressions.

If they're speaking or acting from a warped perspective, they're hurting *themselves*—not you.

When someone confuses truth with falsehood, the truth isn't harmed—only the person who's fallen into error.

Keeping this in mind, turn away any insult or injury with kindness. Remind yourself, "It seems right to them, but they're mistaken."

43
Two Handles

Every situation has two handles—one by which you can safely carry it, and one that's dangerous to grasp.

If a friend treats you unfairly, don't try to pick it up by the *handle of revenge*, or you'll burn your hand!

Reach instead for the *handle of reconciliation*. Remember that this friendship enriches both of your lives, and the relationship is worth keeping.

By this handle, it can be carried.

44
Proper Logic

Here are some examples of illogical conclusions:

"I'm richer than you, so I'm more valuable to society."

"I'm a better speaker than you, so my opinion is more important."

The logical conclusions would be:

"I'm richer than you, so I can buy more things."

"I'm a better speaker than you, so I can more easily share my opinions."

A person's *inside* isn't measured by their *outside*.

45
Don't Rush to Judge

When you catch your mind judging others, stick to the facts.

Did someone bathe quickly? Don't say that they're a slob, only that they washed quickly.

Did someone drink a whole bottle of wine? Don't say that they're a drunkard, only that they drank a lot.

Without access to all of a person's thoughts and motivations, how can you judge them? Don't mistake your assumptions for the truth.

46
Show, Don't Tell

Don't proclaim yourself a philosopher and go around preaching. Show your principles by example.

At a feast, don't stand up and give a speech about moderation. Just partake moderately yourself.

Socrates never pontificated or put on airs. In philosophical conversations, follow his example—ask a lot of questions and listen more than you speak.

If anyone assumes from your silence that you must be ignorant, take it as a compliment. Now you're a true student of philosophy!

Sheep don't spit out grass to show the farmer how much they've eaten. They ruminate on it, digest it, and then display the results in wool and milk.

In the same way, don't spew your undigested ideas. Show the fruits of your studies in *action*.

47
Silent Simplicity

When you restrain your bodily appetites to gain self-control, don't brag about it.

At the dinner table, instead of announcing, "I've given up wine, and so should you," just say, "Only water for me, thanks."

If you think you're austere, remember the poor. They enjoy far fewer comforts, and endure far greater hardships, than you.

Don't make a spectacle of your simplicity, or you defeat the purpose.

48
Be Internally Anchored

Most people swing between elation and despair, tossed about by the currents of circumstances and events.

But philosophers are *internally anchored*.

They take responsibility for their thoughts and emotions. They don't blame anyone or anything for how they think and feel.

They limit their striving to what's within their sphere of power. They accept what's beyond their control, rather than argue with it.

Their only enemies are those things which corrupt their character and disrupt their peace of mind—like greed, fear, envy, and hatred.

When philosophers fail, they correct their course. When they succeed, they smile to themselves.

No matter how accomplished, they consider themselves lifelong students—not masters.

49
Learning to Live

When you hear a teacher boast of being able to understand and interpret difficult philosophical writings, remember—if the philosophers had written clearly and simply, there'd be nothing to brag about.

What do I seek? To know the ways of nature. *Who can help me know the ways of nature?* Great philosophers, presumably. *But I can't understand their writings—who can help me?* Teachers and interpreters.

When a teacher explains the meaning of a difficult text, my response should be to *follow the truths* revealed—not to *follow the teacher* as a guru.

The whole point of learning is to *live well.* Those who put all their focus on reading and interpreting books are academics, not philosophers.

50
Stick to Your Principles

Once you've found a principle, follow it as though it were a law.

Don't worry if others criticize or laugh at you—their opinions aren't your concern.

51
Your Time Is Now

How long will you make excuses for not putting your principles into practice? How long will you wait before following the light of reason wherever it leads?

Are you waiting to find an "infallible" teacher to give you all the answers? Some guru to whom you can hand over your free will? You're responsible for your own life—it's time to take charge.

If you're lazy or halfhearted when it comes to practicing philosophy, you'll be tossed and tormented by external forces till your death.

Starting this moment, choose to act like the worthy and capable person you are. Follow unwaveringly what reason tells you is the best course.

Approach life as your very own Olympic Games. Train thoroughly and act decisively—for one movement can determine the difference between victory and defeat.

Look to Socrates—he continually improved himself in every way, with reason as his guide.

Of course, you and I aren't Socrates. But with effort, we can attain the same virtues as Socrates.

52
Philosophy for Life

In studying philosophy, the *first lesson* is the practical application of principle. The *second lesson* is understanding the reasons behind the principle. The *third lesson* is verifying the principle through logic.

For example:

First, *practice* the principle of Honesty.

Second, contemplate all the *reasons* why telling the truth is better than lying.

Third, use *logic* to show that honesty is the best policy.

Each lesson is valuable, but the first—*practical application*—is the essential foundation.

In most schools of philosophy, alas, they skip the first lesson and spend all their time discussing theory and hypotheticals.

Philosophy is for living, not just learning!

53
Words to Live By

Here are some of my favorite sayings:

> Lead me, Fate, wherever you will,
> and I will cheerfully follow.
> For even if I kick and wail,
> all the same I must follow.
> —CLEANTHES

> Whoever yields to fate becomes wise,
> by learning the laws of heaven.
> —EURIPIDES

> They may kill me, but they can't harm me.
> —SOCRATES

Find your own favorites. Memorize them, keep them close to your heart, and—above all—*live by them!*

FURTHER READING

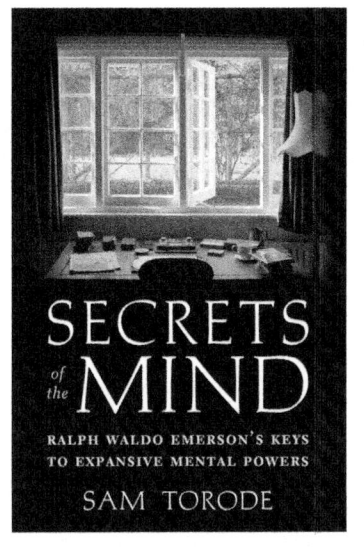

THE MEDITATIONS
An Emperor's Guide to Mastery
MARCUS AURELIUS

SECRETS of the MIND
RALPH WALDO EMERSON'S KEYS TO EXPANSIVE MENTAL POWERS
SAM TORODE

LIVING from the SOUL
THE 7 SPIRITUAL PRINCIPLES OF RALPH WALDO EMERSON
SAM TORODE

AS A MAN THINKETH
21st CENTURY EDITION
the wisdom of JAMES ALLEN
republished by SAM TORODE

www.samtorode.com

Printed in Great Britain
by Amazon